ELY CATHEDRAL

ABOVE: *A view of the cathedral from the south-east.* FACING PAGE: *Around the Octagon are eight sculptured corbels which tell the story of the foundress, St Etheldreda, in stone. The corbel which is illustrated here depicts the consecration of St Etheldreda.*

D0610099

ELY CATHEDRAL

M. S. CAREY, M.A., Dean

The definite history of Ely began in A.D. 673 though the early histories refer to a church at Ely which was consecrated by St Augustine and later destroyed by Penda, King of Mercia. It was in 673 that St Etheldreda, Queen of Northumbria, came to Ely to found a religious community. The great Saxon historian Bede describes it as a nunnery, but almost certainly this was a double monastery of monks and nuns, and, as first Abbess, St Etheldreda ruled over both houses. The life of worship and service to God has continued ever since. The daily round of services is maintained, the educational work goes on in the King's School, thousands of visitors come to the Cathedral in a manner reminiscent of the great medieval pilgrimages, the Cathedral plays its part in the life of the City and the Diocese of Ely.

Our Foundress was a woman of forceful character. Bede describes her thus: 'Now King Egfrid [of Northumbria] took to wife Etheldreda, as was her name, the daughter of Anna, King of the East English, of whom we have often made mention, a man marvellously godly and in all points notable in thought and deed: which same woman had been wedded to another man that is to say to the Prince of the South Gyrwas, named Tondbert, before Egfrid wedded her. But Tondbert dying a little after he took her to wife, she was given to the aforesaid king: with whom she lived twelve years and yet remained always a pure and glorious virgin.'

*

LEFT: *The lovely Galilee Porch, the west entrance of the cathedral, is an exquisite example of Early English architecture, dating from about the time of Magna Carta.*

RIGHT: *This carving is known as the Ely Imps. To find it one must stand on the north side of the choir facing south, at the point where the first and second arches meet above the choir stalls.*

A series of eight remarkable carvings on the capitals of the pillars of the Octagon tells her story. Etheldreda eventually persuaded King Egfrid to release her to become a nun. She was admitted to the community of Coldingham in Northumbria but she had to flee from there to escape Egfrid's attempt to bring her back and so she came to Ely, an island remote and protected by the surrounding fens. The Isle of Ely was her own property, being the dowry of her first marriage to Tondbert. In the year 673 St Wilfred, Archbishop of York, who had been her friend and adviser during her years in Northumbria, installed her as Abbess at Ely. So began the history of Ely which has now run for over thirteen hundred years.

Etheldreda presided over the Community for six years until she succumbed to an epidemic which swept East Anglia; she suffered from a severe tumour in the throat which caused her death in 679. She was buried on 23 June in the community's burial ground in a plain wooden coffin, in accordance with her own instructions.

Her two sisters, Sexburga and Withburga, had also founded religious communities, at Minster in Sheppey and at Dereham in Norfolk. Sexburga was chosen to come from the Isle of Sheppey to be Abbess of Ely. She decided that St Etheldreda's body should be moved into the Church. A white marble coffin was found at Granta, as Cambridge was then called, to contain her body which was exhumed on 17 October 695 and was found to be marvellously preserved from corruption. With much ceremony the re-burial took place in the Saxon church of which nothing remains, though its probable site is on St Cross Green on the north side of the present Cathedral. The shrine quickly became a place of pilgrimage and miracles were associated with it. Sexburga died on 6 July 699. She had once been the wife of Erconbert, King of Kent, and had entered the religious

life when she was widowed. From that marriage there was a daughter named Ermenilda, who was married to Wulfere, King of Mercia. She too was widowed and became a nun at Ely under her Aunt, St Etheldreda. Ermenilda had been chosen to succeed her mother Sexburga at Sheppey when the latter came to Ely as Abbess, and she was now chosen to succeed her mother yet again as Abbess of Ely. So our first three Abbesses were all Anglo-Saxon queens, and this fact is represented by the three crowns in the High Altar frontal

The only object remaining from those Saxon days is the Ovin stone in the south aisle of the nave. This is the

Continued on page 6

LEFT: *The nave, looking east. The Norman columns rise one behind another 72 feet to the roof. The ceiling, always of wood, was painted 1858–65.*

ABOVE: *The unique feature of Ely cathedral: the Octagon. Conceived by Alan of Walsingham, the whole is a masterpiece of engineering and, in both conception and execution, bears the evidence of the highest genius of medieval craftsmen. The main timber structure of the Octagon supports 400 tons of wood and lead.*

base of a cross bearing a Latin inscription in Roman capitals *LUCEM TUAM OVINO DA DEUS ET REQUIEM. AMEN.* ('Thy light to Ovin grant, O God, and rest. Amen'.)

Ovin was Queen Etheldreda's steward, who managed her estates, entered the monastery at Ely and later moved to Lichfield. The stone dates from early in the 8th century. It disappeared for a long time but was discovered by Canon Bentham, the chief historian of Ely, in the 18th century. It was being used as a mounting-block outside an inn at Haddenham. Bentham brought it back to Ely, where it stands in the Cathedral as the sole physical link with this early Saxon period.

The life of the Community continued quietly and faithfully until the latter part of the 9th century. The Fens gave the island good protection and made it almost inaccessible. But in 869 the Danes came from the sea, sacked the house, killed the monks and nuns and left the place a ruin. What kind of life continued after that is obscure, but it seems probable that the place was cared for by some secular clergy.

However, religious life is not destroyed as easily as that. During the reign of King Edgar and the Archbishopric of St Dunstan, there was a great revival of the rule of St Benedict. In 970 Ely was re-founded as a Benedictine monastery for men, with Britnoth as first Abbot. King Edgar granted the foundation a royal charter confirming the Abbey's possessions and privileges. The original charter is one of Ely's most treasured possessions and is kept in the University Library in Cambridge.

Britnoth restored the ruined church and re-established the prosperity of the Abbey. Benefactions of land began to be received in his time. By a not very reputable ruse he contrived to get the body of St Etheldreda's sister, Withburga, away from Dereham and buried it beside the other three members of

★

ABOVE, left: *The Prior's Door opened on to the cloisters, on the far side of which was the Prior's lodging. The door is of late Norman date.*

LEFT: *This base of a cross, called Ovin's Stone, carries us back to the very beginning of Ely's history, for it is the only object remaining from Saxon days.*

that royal family. The Danes continued to be a menace, but another Britnoth, Duke of Northumbria, helped the monastery not only by keeping the Danes at bay until he was killed at Maldon, Essex, but also by his benefactions. A small Latin inscription in his memory is to be seen in Bishop West's Chapel where his bones are laid to rest. The Danish story ends on a happier note, for King Canute came to Ely to celebrate the feast of Candlemas, an event honoured in an old Saxon poem, translated into contemporary English by Dean Stubbs. A musical setting was composed by Dr Arthur Wills, Cathedral Organist, and this carol is now traditionally sung in the Cathedral at Christmas.

Ely, for all its seclusion in the almost impassable fens, was not yet at the end of its turbulent period. After the invasion of William the Conqueror, the last Saxon resistance was based on Ely, under the leadership of Hereward the Wake, a fine soldier with a European reputation. He had the Earls Edwin and Morcar as his allies. But the monks grew weary of his soldiers billeted on them, the privations of the siege and the sequestration of their estates. They sent a deputation to William and disclosed an access to the Isle and the resistance was overcome. The monastery was subjected to severe fines and deprived of much of its land. A Norman Abbot, Theodwin, was introduced, after the death of Thurstan, the last Saxon Abbot, who owed his preferment to King Harold.

Abbot Simeon, appointed by William and accepted by the monks, was eighty-six years old when he was appointed in 1081. He succeeded in getting much of the monastic property returned on the grounds of the original grant to St Etheldreda and the subsequent charter of King Edgar. He regarded the Saxon church as inadequate, and in spite of his years embarked upon the mighty task of building our present church, beginning with the east end. After his death in 1093 William Rufus kept the Abbacy vacant and appropriated to himself the revenues, which caused a serious hold-up in the building work. However, by 1106 the building was sufficiently far advanced to enable a second translation of the body of St Etheldreda to be made. The marble coffin was moved, once again on 17 October, to a shrine to the east of the High Altar. The building work went on steadily until the church was completed in 1189. It is interesting to note the difference between the rather crude arcading still to be seen in the lowest stories of the transepts and the fully developed romanesque work in the south-west transept adjoining the west tower, though the carvings on the capitals of the early pillars are of great interest, being a mixture of Saxon and Norman artistic traditions.

In the south-west transept is some of the finest romanesque work in the country, comparable with that at Durham and at Christ Church Priory in Hampshire. The magnificent nave, which partly borrows its feeling of soaring height from the exceptionally high triforium, provides one of the most stimulating architectural thrills in the world. There have been only five significant alterations to the building from that day to this.

The builders of Ely were fortunate in being able to obtain stone from the quarry at Barnack, near Stamford. This Barnack stone is the hardest limestone to have been quarried in England, and it was brought to Ely by the waterways. Its exceptionally durable quality is well seen in the so-called Prior's Door on the south side of the nave, which dates from about 1150. The glorious carving of Christ in Majesty in the tympanum of this door is another of Ely's great treasures. The surround of the door is intricately carved with the representation of a vine and many fascinating people and wild creatures. The Monks' doorway from the remains of the cloister is of the same date and is another superb example of stone-carving.

In 1109 an event occurred of lasting significance in Ely's history. The Abbot, Hervé le Breton, obtained confirmation from the Pope of his appointment as Bishop of a new diocese of Ely, carved out of the then enormous diocese of Lincoln. He is reputed to have acquired for the new see the lion's share of the monastic lands and revenues, though it must be said that some of his successors turned this to the benefit of the church, which then became a Cathedral, by their remarkable building projects. Furthermore, if Ely had not been an episcopal see at the time of the dissolution of the monastery in 1539, the whole place would almost certainly have joined the company of majestic ruins so widely spread throughout the land. The Bishop continued to be titular Abbot, but the Prior became head of the monastery. One interesting result

ABOVE: *Two of the carved stone heads on the arches round the Octagon. The top one is thought to be Alan of Walsingham's master mason, the lower one Prior Crauden.*

7

is that there is no Bishop's throne in Ely as in most Cathedrals, but the Bishop continues to occupy the Abbot's stall and the Dean, successor of the Priors, occupies the Prior's stall.

Bishop Eustace was the first to use his resources for the benefit of the building when, in the early 13th century, he added the beautiful, delicately worked Galilee porch. If this is correctly dated it is an exceptionally early example of the new style of architecture, known as Early English, which displaced romanesque.

By this time Ely was becoming a famous place of pilgrimage. The city had a licence to hold a fair twice a year around 23 June and 17 October, the two festival days of the Foundress. The fairs still continue. The souvenirs bought at the St Audrey's fairs came to be known, by a corruption of the name, as 'Tawdry', thus contributing a word to the English language. The crowds in the Cathedral became an inconvenience around the shrine, so Bishop Hugh of Northwold, who succeeded to the bishopric of 1229, resolved to extend the church by pulling down the Norman apsidal east end and building the magnificent presbytery of six bays. The dignity and simplicity of this building, of Barnack stone and Purbeck marble (very much the fashion—cf. Westminster Abbey and Salisbury), is pure glory. It was completed in 1252 and was consecrated in the presence of King Henry III and his son, the future Edward I. The shrines of St Etheldreda and the other Abbesses were once more moved on 17 October to their final position until their destruction at the Reformation. The site is marked by a large slate with a beautifully incised inscription in Bishop Hugh's presbytery, that most noble of all the episcopal benefactions.

The concluding phase of medieval Christian culture was marked by a great devotion to Our Lady. In Ely this

*

ABOVE: *The transepts on each side of the Octagon have highly decorated roofs with angel hammer-bearers, carved in the 15th century.*

LEFT: *The Lady Chapel.*

RIGHT: *The screen and choir, seen from the Octagon. Notice the lovely lierne vaulting of the roof which now covers the choir in place of the original Norman roof.*

ABOVE: *These choir stalls were made by Alan of Walsingham for use in the Octagon. They were moved to their present position about 1850. The carved groups under each canopy are nineteenth-century work by Belgian carvers.*

★

LEFT: *Two examples of the 62 superb carvings under the choir stall seats. These examples show 'The Fall, the angel keeping Adam and Eve out of Eden' (above) and two 'religious' with a devil between them (below).*

★

RIGHT: *This is a fine example of one of the sculptured corbels around the Octagon, which tell the story of the foundress, St Etheldreda. Another example appears on the inside front cover of this book.*

was given expression in the founding of the Lady Chapel in 1321 in an unusual position in the angle between the presbytery and the north transept. Before the work had made much progress disaster struck—disaster which was turned into opportunity. The central tower of the Norman church had been ill founded, and on 12 February 1322 it collapsed with a roar like thunder, destroying the Norman choir and severely damaging the abutting bays of the nave and the transepts. One can imagine the feelings of dismay as the community looked at the vast pile of rubble. However, it was fortunate that the community included just then some really remarkable men—Bishop Hotham, Prior Crauden and Alan of Walsingham, the Sacrist, who was in charge of the fabric. They obtained the services of William Hurley, evidently a London man, who in 1336 received the royal warrant as King's Master Carpenter.

Alan of Walsingham wasted no time in clearing away all the rubble. Faced by a great open space, 'he had a moment of supreme creative vision.' Instead of restoring the Norman work, he used the space, 72 feet in diameter, to create the irregular octagon by building eight huge pillars at the corners. He was then confronted with a most difficult roofing problem. Here William Hurley was brought in to advise on the design of the lantern tower. It is a great construction of timber triangles resting on the eight pillars and supporting at their apices the Lantern which rises up sixty feet, each of the corner posts being a single oak tree of 10 tons in weight, between which are the windows which make the whole structure a lantern. The construction has a total weight of some 400 tons, and is so accurately designed that it rests upon the eight pillars with a sheer perpendicular downward thrust. It would be a work of engineering genius in any age. It remains as a supreme example of medieval craftsmanship, unique in the whole of Europe. How right it is that the Octagon and Lantern are frequently called Ely's chief glory. Bishop Hotham's contribution was to restore at his own expense the Norman part of the presbytery. This work was carried out in the decorated style whose distinction from Bishop Hugh's work is easily discerned. This operation attracted the attention of Queen Philippa, wife of Edward III,

who was evidently a visitor to Ely at this time. All these great people are commemorated in the stone carvings of their heads round the Octagon— north west, Alan of Walsingham and William Hurley; north east, King Edward III and Queen Philippa; south east, Bishop Hotham and Prior Crauden. The ceiling of the Lantern culminates in a beautiful carving of Christ in glory, the work of John of Burwell. It is life size, and about 150 feet above the floor.

During all this work the building of the Lady Chapel continued under the direction of a monk called John of Wisbech. Barnack stone (nearly the last of it, since the quarry was worked out in the 15th century) was used, and for the interior, clunch, a local hard chalk very suitable for the astonishingly intricate carving. 'The earliest known record of the purchase of bricks anywhere in England is in the Ely Sacrist Rolls of 1335 and 1337. Some of these or similar bricks are still to be seen in the parapet walls of the Lady Chapel.' (Donovan Purcell, F.R.I.B.A., Surveyor to the Fabric 1960–73.) This beautiful building, with its wide soaring windows, is almost a glass house with a stone frame. The whole interior has a surround of carvings of events, actual and apocryphal, of the life of Our Lady and legendary miracles associated with her. The carving of the two-dimensional ogee curves in the canopies over the stone seats is staggering. The roof is the widest medieval stone vault in England, the span being 46

feet and the construction so delicate that the middle is only 18 inches higher than the sides. Much of the interior was originally painted and the windows contained rather heavy stained glass. At the time of the Reformation, when men over-reacted against medieval devotion, much of it admittedly superstitious, all the beautiful carvings and the windows were smashed to smithereens, no doubt in excessive zeal for the purity of exclusive Biblical truth.

As if all this work were not enough, Crauden also built a charming little chapel, known as Prior Crauden's chapel, which can be seen among the buildings to the south of the Cathedral. What tremendous men they were and what a heritage they left us! Fortunate indeed it was that they were so industrious as to finish all this work between 1321 and 1349 when the Black Death smote England, playing havoc with the economy and really heralding the decline and fall of the medieval period.

The medieval builders had one more, some say disastrous, major trick up their sleeves before the building was to be left as we have it today. Despite the recent memory of the collapse of the Norman central tower, it was decided to build on top of the West Tower a large octagonal belfry with four supporting turrets. This was the fifth and last major alteration to the original Norman church. Whether this belfry was built before or after the collapse of the north-west transept cannot be told, as there is no record of

Continued on page 14

LEFT: *The Presbytery and High Altar. Bishop Northwold built this magnificent Early English addition to the east end to house the shrine of St Etheldreda.*

Work began in 1234 and the relics were placed in their new resting place in 1252. ABOVE: *The nave, looking west. From this view, the west end is so far away*

that even its great arch, which mounts so high above one's head when entering the building, looks quite low and narrow. The nave is 248 feet long.

when the transept fell. That and the construction of the belfry have combined to give Ely's west front, which must have been very splendid, its curiously disproportionate and lopsided appearance, at once so odd and so attractive. The belfry is more than 60 feet high, and the four supporting turrets are even higher. It is in effect a vast wooden cage encased in stone and glass of ingenious and delicate construction. Yet from the beginning it has been too heavy for the Norman work beneath it and has caused great expense to succeeding generations. The work probably began in 1392 under the direction of Master Robert de Wodehirst, the mason.

Even by 1405 defects were apparent, and in 1476 Thomas Peynton was employed 'on strengthening the Western Tower'. This probably meant the construction of the huge stone casing to be seen round the four main pillars, and the sturdy relieving arches beneath the four Norman originals.

As a final fling there were built in the north-east and south-east corners the two chantry chapels of Bishop Alcock and Bishop West, the former an almost vulgar piece of virtuosity in stone, the latter a superbly delicate creation of the early 16th century, with a deep coffered italianate ceiling, a worthy harbinger of the age of humanism and modernity into which Europe was beginning to pass. The construction of Ely Cathedral was complete. Destruction and decay were waiting round the corner. Restoration

and revival were two hundred and fifty years ahead.

King Henry VIII dissolved the monastery in 1539. Certainly some of the monks remained and carried on their worship. The bishopric survived. In 1541 King Henry granted a new charter (still in existence and kept in Cambridge University Library), establishing the 'King's New College at Ely'. It assigned an income to support a Dean, eight canons, 'eight peticanons, four students in divinity, xxiii scholars to be taught grammar, six aged men decayed in the King's wars or service'. The charter also provided for a staff to manage the estates, and for singing men and boys. The chief work of Ely since 673, the daily pattern of the worship of God in the name of Jesus Christ, was to continue.

As reforming enthusiasm waxed hotter in the land the act requiring the 'destruction of all images and reliquaries' was obeyed at Ely on the instructions of Bishop Goodrich, with devasting effect still to be seen, particularly in the Lady Chapel and Bishop West's chapel, and complete dismantling of St Etheldreda's shrine. Very few remains of this shrine can be identified, though a remarkable panel of four 15th-century paintings, probably part of a triptych above the altar of the shrine, is now the property of the Society of Antiquaries in London.

Most of the medieval buildings survived and, with adaptations, are still lived in, forming what is reputed to be the largest collection of medieval

buildings still in daily use in the country. For a while there was even a residual common life, since an early document of the King's Commissioners assigns accommodation to the members of the new foundation and deals thus with the old Refectory: 'The great hall to be for ye petit canons with all the menysters and officers to dine and sup in with the voltes underneath ye same and also the convent kichyn and the litel buttre adjoining to the same with suffic Implementes of Kechyn stuff, botry and napry.' No doubt the introduction of wives and families of the Canons gradually eroded this common life, though it still survives on four occasions in the year, when the Chapter lunch together after two statutory meetings, and on the feasts of St Etheldreda when they entertain the Greater Chapter of honorary canons.

So much for destruction; Oliver Cromwell, so often blamed, can be exonerated as far as the Cathedral is concerned, though the destruction of the cloister buildings and Chapter House is attributed to his period. Cromwell was a tithe farmer to the Chapter and lived in Ely having inherited the leasehold of considerable property from his father. He disliked the chanting of services as being 'unedifying and offensive'. He also despised the preaching. He ordered the choir office to stop and is reputed to have locked the place up for seventeen years, subsequently ordering more frequent and longer sermons to be preached. This is the only break in a continuity of worship for thirteen hundred years.

After the destruction, the decay. No doubt the unsettled 17th century was an impoverished time, and too little

*

LEFT: *An example of the lovely carved bosses in the roof of the presbytery, depicting the Coronation of the Virgin.*

RIGHT: *The Tiptoft monument. This magnificent triple-canopied tomb is in the south choir aisle. John Tiptoft, Earl of Worcester, lies between his two wives. He was beheaded in the Wars of the Roses and buried in a church on Ludgate Hill. His ruthlessness in those wars earned him the title of 'the Butcher', but he was also a man of learning. The Tiptoft family owned wide estates near Ely.*

appears to have been done to maintain the Cathedral. In 1699 the north-west corner of the north transept was restored under the direction, it is said, of Sir Christopher Wren, nephew of Matthew Wren who was Bishop of Ely 1638–67. Certainly the style of the doorway there, as also the entrance to the south cloister, suggests the possibility of this though there is a Chapter resolution to commission Robert Grumbold, a Cambridge mason-architect, who had a close connection with St Botolph's church, Cambridge. The stone used was Ketton, which accords ill with the Barnack stone of the rest of the building. In spite of this work, so bad was the condition that in 1724(?) Daniel Defoe wrote 'some of it is so ancient, totters so much with every gust of wind, looks so like decay, and seems so near it, that whenever it does fall, all that 'tis likely will be thought strange in it, will be that it did not fall a hundred years sooner.' (*Journey throughout the whole of Great Britain*: Defoe.) In 1750 James Essex, the Cambridge architect, was called in to see to repairs. Having referred to the fact that Ely was then known as the Dead See he said of the Cathedral that 'children were sent to play in it on wet days, coal carts were taken along the nave floor because traction there was easier than in the city streets, a farrier's forge occupied the Baptistery and pigeons were bred and shot in the Cathedral' (quoted by Donovan Purcell, F.R.I.B.A., in an article).

Essex has been criticised for his work, but he saved the Cathedral, particularly the Lantern, with great skill. Some of his work in the West Tower remains and is still effective. In this period the medieval stone pulpitum which acted as a screen between the nave and the choir, which still stood under the Octagon, was removed, the 14th-century choir stalls were moved as far eastward as they could go, the Holy Table was placed right against the east wall and a curious plaster screen with an organ on top was sited where the choir stalls now stand. The arrangement was reckoned to be in the name of 'pure religion and true taste', and to provide a fine preaching place. A watercolour painting of the period shows the strange and unsatisfactory arrangement.

All this was not enough to bring the whole building back into good order. William Cobbett wrote slightingly of it and characteristically slanged the Chapter. Watercolour paintings of the time show great blocks of masonry lying about. Then in 1839 Dr Peacock came to Ely as Dean and the great period of restoration began. He set about his work with immense vigour. He improved the order of conducting the worship. The most active period of all was when the work was under the direction of Sir Gilbert Scott. The Essex screen was taken down. The choir stalls were brought to their present position, surely the ideal one. Into the canopies a beautiful set of wood carvings was inserted. They are the work of a Belgian carver of Louvain, depicting Old Testament scenes on the south side and the life of Our Lord on the north.

The nave was given a new floor; the roofs were strengthened, the exterior of the Octagon received its pinnacles; elaborate repairs were carried out to the West Tower. The nave was given a ceiling. In 1858 'a boarded ceiling was put up and painted without fee by Mr L'Estrange of Hunstanton Hall. After his death it was completed (on the same terms) by Mr Gambier Parry of Highnam Court, Gloucestershire' (Atkinson). Though not to everyone's taste, it must surely rank as one of the great Victorian works of church art. The design is based on the early 13th-century ceiling in St Michael's Church, Hildesheim, in Germany.

The windows also date from this period, and have come in for much criticism as bad glass. Nevertheless the west window is beautiful. Most of the

*

LEFT: *This fine ceiling of Bishop West's chantry, built in 1533, blends gothic design and classical ornament.*

RIGHT: *Bishop West's beautiful chantry at the end of the south aisle.*

glass is 16th-century French, with some very skilful adaptation dating from 1853. The great east window convincingly portrays events from the life of Our Lord and is a fine example of 19th-century glazing. In Ely no medieval windows survived, only little fragments. In the 1970s some of these fragments have been restored and fashioned into a delightful window in St Dunstan's chapel by Mr Dennis King of Norwich.

Meanwhile the life of the Cathedral was also being reformed and this reached a height under Dean Harvey Goodwin, later Bishop of Carlisle, so much so that in the 1870s Mr Gladstone described Ely as a 'pattern for the Cathedrals of England'.

In the present century further work has been necessary. In the 1950s the Lantern timbers were found to be badly infected by death-watch beetle. Dean Hankey launched an appeal and the money was raised to restore the Lantern and other roofs. It was also in his time that the Octagon was surely at last, after a delay of six hundred years, put to its ideal use as the site for an altar. The existing furniture, designed by Mr George Pace, F.R.I.B.A., was placed there in 1973. The whole arrangement provides a perfect setting for Liturgy in a way which accords excellently with contemporary Eucharistic practice.

But once again the West Tower was to cause the greatest trouble. A survey conducted in 1971–2 under direction of Mr Donovan Purcell, F.R.I.B.A., Surveyor to the Fabric, revealed a most serious condition in spite of the work by Essex and Scott. Restoration had to be put in hand at once and yet another appeal was launched. A very thorough restoration indeed was carried out in 1973 and 1974 with the most up-to-date techniques available. The work began under the direction of Mr Purcell, with Professor Jacques Heyman, Professor of Engineering at Cambridge University, as consultant. The firm of Rattee and Kett of Cambridge

*

LEFT: *This photograph shows the tomb of William de Luda of Louth, through which can be seen the tomb of Bishop Redman.*

RIGHT: *Here, at the end of the north aisle, can be seen the elaborate stone carving of Bishop Alcock's chantry. The stone staircase on the right is modern; it leads to the organ loft.*

have effected these most elaborate repairs at a cost of some £280,000. Mr Purcell did not live to see the great work complete, as he died in December 1973 and the direction passed to Mr Peter Miller, F.R.I.B.A., whom the Chapter appointed as Surveyor to the Fabric. It might be tempting providence to suggest that a final solution has been achieved to a problem which has been troublesome for five hundred years, but such substantial and first-class work ought to endure. It is certainly on a scale to match the heroic efforts of the past, and exemplifies the determination of a large number of people who have been benefactors to preserve Ely Cathedral as one of the great national, indeed European, treasures.

Behind all this history of the building lies its life. The most important part of this is largely hidden, as was the intention of our original Foundress when she came from Northumbria to the seclusion of the Isle of Ely. Our Lord advised 'when you pray go into your room and shut the door'. Who would choose to make a parade of his devotional life?

Throughout all the vicissitudes, in times of quiet as well as in times of turbulence, the central work of worship has gone steadily on, with the one brief Cromwellian interruption, for thirteen hundred years. It is fitting that in such a magnificent setting the worship should be offered with the greatest beauty possible. Henry VIII's provision for singing men and boys still applies and the work of the Choir continues to be at the heart of the life here. In the summer there may be crowds to hear and join in the worship; on cold winter days there may be no one. It makes no difference; the offering of the *opus dei* is for God and as much care is taken in the solitary times as in the crowded times. Choirs need music. In 1907 a very fine organ was placed in the north choir triforium. Built by Harrison of Durham, it set a pattern for English organ building which lasted fifty years. By 1974 the organ had reached the term of its life and a most generous benefactor has enabled it to be rebuilt, a task undertaken by Harrisons, the original builders.

Education has always been a special concern of religious communities, and without doubt children were entrusted to the care of St Etheldreda. The Benedictine foundation of the 10th century included a school and King Edward the Confessor is reputed to have been one of the pupils. The school continued in Henry VIII's new foundation and has been maintained as the King's School. It is now an independent school of some five hundred pupils, seniors and juniors, boarding and day, boys and girls, the school having become co-educational in 1970, which would surely have given satisfaction to our foundress. The Chapter provide bursaries to enable the choristers to attend the school.

Not all the hundreds and thousands of visitors to the cathedral come strictly as pilgrims in the old sense, although increasingly parties of Christians are doing this. Yet a good many

*

LEFT: *The Royal Air Force memorial window in the north choir aisle.*

RIGHT: *The interior of Bishop Alcock's chapel. The effect of such richness and complexity of stone carving is almost overwhelming. A theme of the carving is a cock, sometimes in a design of vine tendrils. This is a reference to the Bishop's name: his rebus, or device, is a cock standing on a globe, depicted in glass on either side of the west entrance to the chapel. Bishop Alcock was a great prelate, Chancellor of Edward IV and the founder of Jesus College, Cambridge. He built his chantry in 1488 and died 12 years later.*

who come just for an outing find that the place lays hold of them in some way and the outing becomes a pilgrimage. When this is so, the hidden inner life of witness to Jesus Christ has been fulfilled.

A cathedral is often called the Mother Church of the Diocese. In it the Bishop has his *cathedra*, chair, stall or throne, as the symbol of his spiritual leadership of the part of Christ's church committed to his care. From time to time the church people travel across the fen lands, drawn towards this church, crowning the hill like a great ship riding upon the sea, as it has been described. They may come for special services, for conferences, for times of quiet prayer, for gatherings of many kinds, but always they come because the cathedral is in some sense theirs, and a place where they can feel at home.

Wherever you may go in Ely, you cannot escape the cathedral as it dominates the scene. Perhaps it was the religious community which in the first place caused Ely to be known, as a town and city. The cathedral is adjacent to the High Street and equal to it in length. The relationship between cathedral and the secular community has had its ups and downs. A particular down occurred in the Littleport Riots of 1816, when half-starved labourers marched on Ely from Littleport, causing much trepidation. The Bishop at that time had palatinate jurisdiction over the Isle, so the subsequent condemnation of the ringleaders, three to be hanged, others sent to Botany Bay, caused deep local resentment. Dean Harvey Goodwin did much to allay this by playing a leading part in social reform in the town. In 1973, when the 13th centenary of the Foundation was

*

LEFT: *A view of the north choir aisle gateway leading to the Octagon.*

RIGHT, top: *Crauden's chapel was built by Alan of Walsingham for the use of Prior Crauden in 1324. It has been described as 'one of the most curious and valuable Decorated remains in the country'.*

RIGHT: *This great gate of the Abbey through which so many historical personages must have passed is called The Porta. It was built by Prior Walpole in 1394 and has served many purposes in its time: a prison and courthouse; a brewery and a residence for lay clerks.*

celebrated, City and Cathedral entered into a true partnership to make a memorable fiesta of worship and celebrations. A monastery needed a high wall and a great gateway to mark its dedication to a particular way of life, but the motto for 1973 was 'With the help of my God I will leap over the wall' (Ps. 18 v.29). The Centenary culminated in the visit of Her Majesty the Queen, who attended Divine Service in the cathedral on 25th November. She honoured Ely by Letters Patent granting to it the use of the style 'City', and the new City Council became entitled to elect a Mayor for the first time.

The School was granted the right to appoint 12 girls as Queen's Scholars to balance the King's Scholars of Henry VIII's foundation.

In this brief History of Ely Cathedral it has been possible to name a few of the significant men and women who did much to benefit the place. We are indeed thankful for them. But we are also thankful for the multitude of unknown people who have served here as 'religious', as craftsmen making beautiful things often in inaccessible places where they are very rarely seen, as musicians, as worshippers and as benefactors. Thank God for them all, for without them there would be nothing here worth visiting. 'Some there be who have no memorial', but 'if you require a memorial look around'. 'Most of all we are thankful to St Etheldreda. Not for the first time, nor, we pray, for the last, has one dedicated life flowered into such a glorious heritage' (Dean Hankey). The seed planted by St Etheldreda in 673 has grown into a massive tree. From time to time it has needed pruning and lopping, but the tree still flourishes and its life and fruit remain true to its original roots.

★

LEFT: *From Saxon days the monks had, among their many activities, a school for boys and when the monastery was dissolved, Henry VIII required the new foundation to continue this important work. School houses are scattered around the precincts of the cathedral and most of them date from the Middle Ages. King School, shown here, has grown greatly in size and its equipment has been designed to meet the needs of the present day.*

BACK COVER: *A view of the cathedral from the south-east.*

Acknowledgments

All the colour pictures in this book are by S. W. Newbery, Hon.F.I.I.P., F.R.P.S., with the exception of the front cover which is by Woodmansterne Ltd. The black-and-white pictures are by Arthur W. Kerr, F.I.I.P., F.R.P.S., with the exception of six taken by S. W. Newbery.

The writer wishes to acknowledge help from the following sources: The Liber Eliensis. *Bentham:* History and Antiquities of the Conventual and Cathedral Church of Ely. *Dean Stubbs:* Historical Memorials of Ely Cathedral. *Dean Hankey:* Ely Cathedral. *Donovan Purcell, F.R.I.B.A.:* Article in Era, Journal of the Eastern Region of the Royal Institute of British Architects, *Dec. 1968:* 'The Stones of Ely Cathedral'. *Thomas Dinham Atkinson:* An Architectural History of the Benedictine Monastery of St Etheldreda at Ely. *Stewart:* Ely Cathedral. *George Zarnecki:* Early Sculpture of Ely.

The 'Friends of Ely Cathedral'

This is an association of people who help to maintain and beautify the Cathedral: minimum subscription £1 p.a. If you are interested please write to the Hon. Secretary, the Deanery, Ely, CB7 4DN

SBN 85372 069 X

As-tu lu bien attentivement ?

C'est ce qu'on va voir...

Essaie de répondre aux questions suivantes.

1. Comment Rosanne a-t-elle été invitée au bal du prince ?
a) Le prince lui a téléphoné.
b) Le prince lui a envoyé une lettre.
c) Le prince est passé la chercher sans l'inviter.

2. Combien y a-t-il de variétés de pizzas au buffet du prince ?
a) 56.
b) 48.
c) 44.

3. Quels sont les jours où les ogres n'ont pas le droit de manger des gens ?
a) Le mardi et le samedi.
b) Le mardi et le jeudi.
c) Du lundi au vendredi.

4. Pourquoi Rosanne et le prince tombent-ils dans les pommes ?
a) Ils ont fait trop de tartes.
b) Leurs casques se sont cognés l'un contre l'autre alors qu'ils allaient s'embrasser.
c) Ils ont eu trop peur.

Tu peux vérifier tes réponses en consultant le site Internet des éditions Dominique et compagnie, à : www.dominiqueetcompagnie.com/apasdeloup.

À cette adresse, tu trouveras des questions supplémentaires, des jeux, des informations sur les autres titres de la collection, des renseignements sur l'auteure et l'illustrateur et plein de choses intéressantes !

La série Première Classe
Des livres écrits avec des élèves du primaire

Le scénario de cette histoire a été élaboré en groupe par la classe de première année de Nancy Lévesque, à l'école Alphonse-Desjardins de Montréal, lors d'une rencontre littéraire animée par Carole Tremblay.

L'auteure a rédigé le texte qu'elle a ensuite soumis aux élèves afin de recueillir leurs commentaires.

Merci à madame Lévesque et, surtout, aux jeunes auteurs pour leur imagination et leur participation enthousiaste à ce projet.

François Barsalo-Chamberland
Nadine Bastien
Samuel Daoust
Naïla Drouin
Nikie-Elmara François
Malaurie-Océanne Gauvin
Xavier Guertin
Imane Kaddour
Anabelle Moussignac
Kevin Jesus Munoz
Aissatou Ndiaye
Charles-Éric Senez
Maha Silini
Janique Trinidade-Bruyère